Praise For A

"There is catalytic power in authenticity, transparency, and vulnerability. It is enough to crack a hole in the ironclad shroud of shame, a hidden affliction that has long been encoded into the DNA of Korean Americans. As you read *A is for Authentic*, you'll recognize yourself in the author's voice and discover unforeseen catharsis."

Josephine M. Kim, Ph.D., LMHC, NCC

Faculty, Harvard University

"Jeanie Chang's journey as a Korean American woman reveals what it means to be the child of striving, loving, demanding parents. Her emotional journey was relegated to the back burner for so many years, but now bursts forth with awareness and compassion, ready to help others on their own journeys. This book will inspire you to get in touch with your inner life."

Ravi Chandra, M.D., D.F.A.P.A.

Psychiatrist and Author, Facebuddha:
Transcendence in the Age of Social Networks

"*A is for Authentic* is an empowering experience. We get an intimate look into one person's life journey from stress, feelings of inadequacy, and hopelessness to the excitement of self-discovery, the freedom of self-acceptance, and a life of hope. It is also a guide to your own life journey. It is a must-read for all teens and young adults and especially for Asian Americans who are particularly vulnerable to the demons of high expectations and feelings of inadequacy."

Paul J. Kim

Founder and CEO of LaSalle Asset Management, and Aventis Asset Management and former Chair of Council of Korean Americans

"Jeanie does an excellent job of explaining the hardship and expectations that come from being an Asian American. Our generation is strictly unique from any other generations that came before us. Often, we struggle to find our identity in America, but we find ourselves also unable to connect with our parents' heritage and culture from Asia. This book also highlights the importance of speaking up on Asian mental health, which is frequently overlooked in our culture. We have to recognize it and acknowledge it in order to break down the stigmas of mental health within Asian culture. If you are a first-generation or second-generation Asian in America or a new country, please read this book!"

Bryan Pham

Co-Founder & CEO, Asian Hustle Network

"Jeanie does an incredible job explaining what tiger parenting is, the effects that it can have on children. and how it may dramatically shape their perspective during both childhood and adulthood years. The book helps us break down the model minority stereotype and why we sometimes think we need to be a certain way to meet the level of expectations other people have for us. Mental health is rarely talked about in Asian culture. It's important for us to read *A is for Authentic* because it helps us recognize that there is a lot of strength in showing our emotions and responding to our mental health. Jeanie's book is must-read."

Maggie Chui

Co-Founder & COO, Asian Hustle Network

A is for Authentic

Not for Anxieties or for Straight A's

Book 1 in the Cultural Confidence™ Series

A is for Authentic

Not for Anxieties or for Straight A's

Book 1 in the Cultural Confidence™ Series

A Memoir by Jeanie Y. Chang, LMFT

A is for Authentic: Not for Anxieties or for Straight A's

Published by The DP Group, LLC., PO Box 584, 150 Wrenn Drive, Cary, NC 27512, United States

ISBN: 978-1-949513-23-3

Library of Congress Control Number: 2021900296

Printed in the United States of America.

First printing edition 2021.

Book Cover Design by Gina Pham

www.yourchangeprovider.com

This book is dedicated to my loving husband of 23 years, Jonathan Chang, who makes me feel cherished. Without his unending patience and support, the book may not have ever been written since he was the one who suggested I write it in the first place.

Table of Contents

Preface

My Message to You

I hope to provide a brave space here and call you forward in being courageous to discover and be your authentic self, which is a journey of life seasons. It took a lot of courage for me to be brave (just saying!). I try to lead by example so I can convey the authenticity in my passion for the work I do in the mental health field.

For the first time in my life, I am very proud of who I am. Sure, I've been proud of my children, my husband, and what they do and who they are. However, it's challenging to say you're proud of yourself for being yourself. I love being Korean American. I love being a wife and a mother of four. I love being a mental health clinician.

This book about my own identity journey, which is still going strong, is about embracing Cultural Confidence™, an intentional, meaningful practice about having healthy emotionality in our lives through realizing the powerful intersections of identity, mindfulness, resilience, and mental health. I am learning to endure the imperfections of my cultural heritage; emboldening me to cultural confidence™, which forges a path to impactful change for transformation.

Introduction

Years ago, my life story did not make sense to me. I could not find a reason why I had to have the story that I did. I grew up as a second-generation Korean American under the guide of "tiger parents." My home environment was incredibly stressful, and the expectations were extremely high. The resulting impact left me feeling that I was never good enough.

Today, I can honestly say that was never the case. Now I embrace my upbringing. But it took me years to get to this point. It is as if my experiences growing up with all the challenges that I faced were a bridge that led me to where I am today. I do not view those times as horrible, as I did at one time. I can see now how they prepared me for my purpose in life.

I am now a Licensed Marriage and Family Therapist (LMFT). I work with adolescents, families, and many diverse organizations to strengthen the family system, reduce the effects of trauma, and help people build resilience, manage fears, and become their true selves.

I believe there is a space of time in each of our lives that is for self-discovery. Perhaps multiple spaces. How can we truly know ourselves without it? From the time I could feel, I always felt anxiety. I am familiar with what stress and anxieties feel like and how they affect lives. I would even go as far as to say stress can play the role of a thief if you let it, robbing you of moments of happiness.

As you will realize when you read this book, my whole life was a preparation stage for my moment of becoming who I am today. And that is true in your life, too. "Becoming" does not necessarily mean you arrive at your destination in life. It is an unfolding process that reveals mysteries about yourself. It is exciting to finally behold who you are as a person and know that you have something to contribute to the greater world!

My hope is that my message through this book encourages those who experienced a stressful upbringing and past traumas, as I did. I want you to know that your anxieties and pressures do not have to last forever. I challenge you to open your heart and mind as I share with you my process of "becoming" so you can succeed in your journey, too.

PART 1

Influences and Impacts
of Upbringing

As a licensed mental health professional, I think about how children take on their parents' anxiety. Stressful and tense is how I describe my childhood. As early as the young age of three, I recall experiencing the feeling of anxiety. Even babies can feel their parents' anxieties. This is why now, as a therapist, I strongly advocate to parents to work on their stressors.

I grew up in a loving Christian home. But at age 14, while alone at home on a Friday night, I stood in the bathroom holding twenty pills in my hand. All I could think about in that moment was how much of a disappointment I was for my family.

The pressure and stress of my environment and my parents' expectations for me left me feeling fearful all the time because I felt so inadequate. Perhaps people who watched me thought I was impressive. But on the inside, I was falling apart.

Chapter I

A Tiger Cub

I grew up as a second-generation Korean American. My parents brought me to the United States from Seoul Korea when I was just four months old. I recall them describing how difficult it was. My mother even told me she hoped to wait to have children after their arrival in the U.S. so she could build herself a small career in interior design. So, she was not too keen on being a young mom in a new country and having to raise me on her own while my father was a medical resident. Now, as an adult, I cannot imagine coming to a new country to live and barely speaking the language. My parents were very well educated, but that did not lessen the efforts they had to make to thrive in a totally new country, culture, and environment.

My mom grew up extremely well-off, and my dad grew up fairly poor. They were partnered together by a matchmaker in Korea. Despite my father's lower social status, he was definitely approved because he graduated at the top of his class from the best university and medical school. He attended Seoul National University, which is considered the "Harvard" of Asia. This was the only way he was accepted into my mom's exceedingly high upper-class family. Class is especially important in traditional Korean culture.

Both my parents grew up in Christian homes, and that is also the way they raised my sister and me. To this day, I hold that this as the saving grace of our family. There was a struggle between the Korean cultural values and Christian values; but in the end, Christianity won. This Christian faith flowed in the darkest moments in my life and is what saved me.

I am the oldest, so my experience was different than that of my sister. The pressures and expectations were much higher for me. I do not believe she would disagree. I felt suffocated all the time—like I was constantly walking on eggshells—especially when my dad came home from work. I feared he would ask about my grades or how I was doing with my schoolwork.

My mom told me that when I was baby through the preschool years, I cried when around my father because I did not recognize him. He was super busy in medical residency and then building his medical practice. I do not remember that part of my life. But I recall that my father was a workaholic. He wanted to be successful as a neurologist in the U.S. So, I did not see a lot of him in my early years.

Yet, both my parents were very present in my life. They were what is known as "tiger parents." The term "tiger mom" came from Yale Law School professor Amy Chua in 2011 when she wrote her memoir. Following that, came the term, "tiger parents." I did not know how to describe my own parents while I grew up; but as an adult, when I heard the term "tiger parents," it was fitting.

Both terms are largely a Chinese American concept, but today they also are well-known stereotypes (in various cultures) for demanding parents who push their children to high levels of achievement. A stereotype of Jewish tiger moms, for instance, is that they push their children to excel academically for professional careers such as doctors or lawyers. Another example of a tiger mom is how some of Hollywood's film stars pushed their children into acting careers. Fathers also exhibit tiger-parenting behaviors.

Tiger parents are very authoritarian, like dictators. It is their way or the highway. For me that meant all work and no play. I had to achieve to the highest in both academics and music. There was no exception. A lot of effort and practice was set as a requirement to ensure my success. I cannot recall childhood moments where I just played and had fun. I am not saying there were none, but I cannot recall any. Going to elite schools, then coming home studying for so many hours on schoolwork and music was the Korean way.

In the Korean culture, showing emotions was not encouraged. Every time I had a music competition, I felt so nervous that I felt I needed to vomit. But I could not tell anyone. The piano was my main instrument. I also played the clarinet. As with everything else, I had to be the best, nothing less than first chair.

One time my emotional state got so bad that I hid my report card. I got a B, but I also got a C in Art. I hated Art class. I got spanked, but I was not sure if it was due to the grade or the fact that I hid my report card.

I got the message early in life that Koreans are supposed to excel in the areas of science and math. I struggled in both when I entered high school and felt so lost. I questioned whether I belonged. My family on my mom's side were all high achievers. All her siblings were doctors.

I had to receive straight A's in school, especially since I was told my cousins did. My cousins were brilliant. I was often compared to them. I resented this while growing up and dreaded our family reunions each summer where we spent a week together. It was comparison after comparison of each child, and I just knew I could not measure up. It was not that I was a terrible student or not talented in music. In fact, I was pretty decent as a student and played the piano at an advanced level. Alas, it was not good enough.

I remember experiencing panic attacks before each summer vacation, which to me is super sad since every child should look forward to their summer breaks. However, my aunts and uncles would schedule an annual recital for all of us to play our instruments in front of each other. Looking back, those experiences were traumatic. My heart still stops when I hear an adult asking a child or adolescent to play instruments or "put on a show" for family members. All my life, I grew up feeling so "less than," not good enough; so, I wished I could be anything but Korean.

I was blessed to have a stay-at-home mom, which is a privilege that I realize today. At the time, I did not always want her at home because, when I got home from school, I just wanted time to rest and relax. I felt like I could never do that that because that was being "lazy or unproductive." I also knew the minute I got home, it was time to work even more what with homework, extra work, and practicing piano for at least an hour.

I admired latchkey kids and thought it was so cool that they had parents who worked and were not there when they arrived home after school. I wanted that freedom that I assumed they experienced. The grass is always greener on the other side.

I cringe even recalling these memories because it triggers unpleasant and anxious feelings. My parents were NOT abusive in any way. But my upbringing by tiger parents made me question my state of being acceptable in so many areas. I constantly thought that whatever I did was not good enough, so I did not want to talk to my parents about anything. It was a consistent state of hyper-vigilance, which I now know is associated with PTSD (Post Traumatic Stress Disorder).

I did not get into trouble just at home. My personality has always been outgoing and talkative. So, I remember times in grade school when I got in trouble because my teachers said I talked too much in class. For some reason, that is a fond memory because, you see, I was not able to express myself at home. It did not feel safe. My talkativeness was another part of me that was not the Korean way.

I got blasted a lot on what my parents' thought was bad behavior such as talking too much or disagreeing. I was very verbose with my parents and, yes, at times disrespectful, as any child can be. I got the sense early on that, as a Korean, I was to be quiet, docile, and put my head down. But that is not the authentic me; it is literally the exact opposite of who I am.

I know my parents loved me. But I cannot recall my mom saying the words "I love you" to me while growing up. I may have heard it when I left for college. My parents parented the way they were parented, having been born and raised in Korea. They did not know another way to parent.

But I know it made me not want to be Korean. If being Korean meant having to get straight A's and be stressed out all the time, I was willing to leave it. This was my mentality growing up. I strongly disliked everything about the Korean culture.

The older I got, the worse it got and the stricter my parents became—because I started pushing back. As a teen, life became difficult on so many more levels for me. I experienced such an identity crisis: me versus self, me versus parents, me versus the Korean culture, me versus my Korean elders, etc.

I went to a very elite and difficult private school from first grade to my senior year. In Korea, it is what Korean parents view as the number one thing to do, as it was the way of providing the best for one's child, especially when it came to education. But my school was snobby and had too many cliques, which for me, was another stressful environment besides home.

Even so, I so wanted to be like my friends at school. I lived in a predominately white neighborhood, so the school I went to was not really diverse. A lot of my friends were tall and blond, and I wanted to be that way too. It did not seem extremely popular to have dark hair and Korean eyes like mine.

On top of not really feeling I belonged, I had little to no social life. Though I got to go to my senior prom, there was no going to birthday parties or social gatherings of any sort while I grew up. Many times, my friends asked me why I did not go to a school function or party. I had no problem letting them know it was my parents' doing, not mine. It was clear how I felt being Korean American.

Today, my parents are quite different, and sometimes I do not recognize them. They still have the "tiger" edge, but it is nowhere near what it used to be.

My dad is now an ordained pastor. After I grew up, I learned a part of his story when he asked me to edit his paper for his ordination. My dad's mom was ill while he grew up. He now shares in his testimony that he promised her he would become the best doctor during his residency in the US and would go back to Korea and cure her.

Well, he did not return to Korea right away. Instead, he got established in the U.S. and decided to stay because my sister and I had adapted to life in America. He wanted us to have the life that was best for us. I was eight, and my sister was five. I viewed his decision as a sacrifice.

Shortly after he made the decision not to move back to Korea, his mother suffered a massive stroke that left her paralyzed for the rest of her life. She could not speak or walk. He blamed himself at first, but eventually he forgave himself. Because he was a neurologist, he was able to be her doctor for one month. I recall my father going to Korea and taking care of her as a medical doctor just like he promised.

When he shared this in his testimony, it brought me to tears. When you are young, you do not think of your parents as "human," but I saw my dad's vulnerability in that experience. I remember that was a turning point in our nuclear family. After my father returned from Korea, he was a changed man. He was less of a workaholic and more engaged with our family (much to my chagrin because it meant more focus on what I was not doing well. He also grew more dedicated to the Christian faith and church.

The pressure and stress of my environment and the expectations left me feeling fearful all the time because I felt I was so inadequate. Perhaps those who observed me might have thought I was impressive. But on the inside, I was falling apart.

This sets the stage for Chapter 2. It shares the story of one of the darkest times in my life. My Christian faith grounded me; without it, I would not have survived that dark time, nor would I be the person I am today.

Today, I am a happy person. And I embrace my Korean culture and learned to appreciate it. But it took many years to get to this point of authenticity. You, too, can learn how to change your life from darkness and anxiety to happiness and wellness and embrace your authenticity. The rest of my story shares insights in how I changed. It is a journey you can follow in your own life.

I believe there is a space of time in each of our lives that is for self-discovery. Perhaps multiple spaces. How can we truly know ourselves without it? You must give yourself permission to feel and discover who you are rather than who someone says you are.

Chapter 2

Awakening

J ust like the dawn ends the darkness and awakens us to a new day, the dark, traumatic times in our lives can lead to an awakening to self-actualization.

Throughout my life's journey, I am a student of my own life. While stress and high expectations were consistently present in my life while growing up, I was always in search of my identity.

My darkest moment came three weeks before I was to compete in the largest piano competition in my life. I was a freshman in high school and struggled with some of my grades, especially in science class. Since it was science, I could not imagine asking for help. After all, what Asian does poorly in science?

There I was at age fourteen, standing in the bathroom, holding at least twenty pills in my hand. It was a Friday night, and I was home alone. My parents expected me to stay home and practice piano while my family was at church. But all I could do in that moment was think about how much of a disappointment I was for my family, and how not "perfect" I was, compared to all the success of my family members. I just was not good enough and felt that I could never be.

I stood there, building up what I thought was a logical case to swallow those pills in my hand, while thinking how convenient it was that my dad is a doctor and I had access to the pills. Some of those pills were neurological samples. Swallowing those pills seemed to be a simple way to end what I perceived as a failure: my life.

Please understand, as I mentioned in Chapter 1, I grew up in a loving Christian home and was not unhappy. But the squelching of my emotions was extremely stressful. All those moments when I felt compared to everyone and hearing my parents indicating their disappointment in me rang true in that dark moment that Friday night. I reached my max of stress. It was too much to handle.

Layer by layer, the pressures of my fourteen years of life formed a reason within me to end my life before it really started. I figured I would take as many pills as possible until I fell unconscious and, hopefully, with little to no pain. I recall seeing at least twenty pills in both of my palms and a big glass of water to chug them all down.

But in my darkest moment as an adolescent, just when I was about to swallow all the pills, I heard the sweetest voice. The voice said, "Jeanie, you're doing the right thing. Go ahead and take those pills because you do not deserve this stress. Take them and everything will be fine."

I thought, "Oh, good. I am getting a confirmation...from ...God?" In that split second, I faltered and hesitated. Then a powerful thought went through my mind. In all my years of growing up in a Christian home and going to Sunday School, of course, I learned something about God. He would not want me to end my life. Rather, He would want me to live my best life, and He would give me the strength to do so.

As I ruminated on this, questioning whether the voice I heard was God's voice, I felt a loving warm embrace from behind. I can still strongly recall the heat radiating from that embrace and the enormous amount of love I felt in that moment. It was the best back hug you could ever imagine getting. To this day, I have not received a back hug as powerful as that one, even from my husband.

In that dark moment, God came to me with the most loving embrace to give me power to sustain myself. I tell you this firmly: Gone was my overwhelming stress, fear, and that feeling of not being good enough. In its place was strength. I saw myself with a cape, and my hair was pretty and flowing behind me and felt I could take on the world.

As I felt this strength, I felt a tingling sensation in my hands and arms. It was surreal. I watched as God led me to put all those pills one by one back into their appropriate bottles. In that out-of-body experience, I watched my arms move and my hands putting those pills back where they belonged, and the thought of ending my life was shut permanently from that day forward. It was clear to me that the voice I heard that night telling me to take my life was not from God.

As God's warm embrace slipped away, I remember feeling such excitement and went straight to the piano. I told myself, "You can do this." I finally found my own voice. I was like the Energizer Bunny in battery advertisements: I kept going and going. In fact, that became my nickname later. I practiced my heart out, and when my family returned, I was still going. I remember my parents looking impressed.

I remember after that, I went upstairs and pulled out my science book and thought: If I work hard, I can do it and get straight A's. I felt at that moment that I could do anything if I worked hard enough.

My perspective shifted in that dark moment. I stopped allowing the fear of not feeling good enough overtake me as before. During the following three weeks, I was in beast mode, studying to raise my grades and practicing for the piano competition. By the way, I was runner-up in that competition!

In my darkest moment, my Christian faith saved me. All those years of learning about God formulated a firm belief about who He is; and, in that moment, He proved himself to be all that I learned. In God's eyes, I am unique; He does not compare me to anyone else, nor was He concerned about my grades, my being perfect, or my stressful efforts for accomplishments.

God was present in that dark moment. He embraced me, and I was able to be myself. And He gave me strength, and I was able to work hard. To this day, when feelings of inadequacy come, I am reminded of my dark moment that Friday night; and I take note and then gain empowerment toward my own self-efficacy. It was like I became a new person, going down a trajectory, a fork in the road that God blessed me to follow. I never let that dark moment define me; but it is a reminder of my vulnerability and how I need to face my feelings of perfectionism each day in my work and my parenting.

What an exciting experience it is to finally behold who you are as a person, someone who has something to contribute to the greater world! The revelation of your purpose burns like a fire that cannot be consumed.

Chapter 3

The Imposter Syndrome

The realization of my existence, my purpose, came at 2:00 a.m. one night after I had my fourth child. But I struggled to realize my purpose for many years before that.

For years, I was overly ambitious at working in jobs that did not fulfill me. I was good at what I did and practiced being the best. But there was a space in my heart that was not satisfied from what I did. Some of the things I did were only to appease my parents, my extended family, and hopefully make them proud of me. Deep inside, I was haunted by the young girl in me who never felt accepted or fulfilled. It was hard to help her. Beneath the buried layers were my desires waiting to be exposed.

I was plagued with the "imposter syndrome," a collection of feelings of inadequacy that persist despite evident success. I think it happens more so when people are successful.

They question, "Am I really supposed to be that successful?" I really did not feel it until recent years while trying to define my own success. Many Asian Americans openly express their struggle with imposter syndrome, and I struggle with it often enough to keep myself humble.

I was in the fourth grade when I decided I wanted to do something different. I had that drive; it was also in my DNA. There were many successful doctors in my family, but that was not the route I wanted to take.

I decided to be a news anchor. I liked my voice and the fact that I could speak well and enunciate words well. My goal was to be the number-one news anchor in the world. I remember telling my parents that, and they liked the idea of my being number one. Of course, it is the Asian way to do things.

When I first started my broadcast career, I loved my job. I worked at the Associated Press Broadcast News Center, and we covered the President Clinton scandal. I loved being a part of the twenty-four-hour news. Where I realized that this career did not work for me is when I would leave work and go home. During that time, I was engaged to the man who is now my husband, and I was happy in my relationship. But, otherwise, I felt like I had no life; I felt unfulfilled.

At the time, I was in my twenties and already felt burnout brewing. Although I had such an ambition to make it to the top in the broadcast world, it did not feel right to continue this way. My work started to define me, almost too much. I lost some relationships during that time because I was too busy. For the sake of what I did not realize back then was the future state of my mental health, I made a pointed decision to leave the journalism field. My decision was much to my parents' chagrin, despite my being in the position of moving up quickly.

I knew I had to pivot quickly to look good on paper and please my parents, so I decided to go to business school. It was a 180-degree turn, but the "Asian-American thing" to do is to look good. My parents said, "OK, fine, go to business school."

I went to business school, truly disliked it, and cried through it. It was not me. Even so, I had to finish and look good. So, I completed my master's degree at Johns Hopkins University, and my family did not suffer in the process.

I had three kids during my time in business school; they were my priority. I ended up using my business degree for a hot second as a marketing media consultant and director of media for a hair products company. But I still felt unfulfilled.

I was a full-time mom at the time, but back then I ignored the power of my family grounding me. I accomplished things in my family that I did not appreciate until later. I did not acknowledge that it was part of my life journey. I remember getting comments like "You have a nice family" and thinking, "Yeah, that is nothing." It was not good enough. I questioned what I was accomplishing. What was I doing with my life?

It is not that I was not happy; rather, I downplayed everything I did as a mother. I always had in the back of my head that I would do something one day that would be as good as being a doctor or lawyer. But at the same time, I also knew I wanted to take care of my kids in the best way possible. Due to my competitive nature, I knew that I could not be a working mom and raise young kids; I knew I would have left my kids in the wayside to build a career.

Thinking back, I got a glimpse of my true purpose while in business school. I was a little older than the students there at the time, so I was the person they came to for counseling and advice. As I raised my kids, I always gave advice and counseling to other moms. I successfully sleep-trained my kids when they were six weeks old, so a lot of moms contacted me for advice on that among other issues that stressed them. I enjoyed counseling them, providing feedback and advice, and even interventions at times. In fact, moms around the country called me for advice. The moms would wish they were like me. I could relate: We often want to be in a different spot than where we are.

The realization of my existence, my purpose came at 2:00 a.m. after I had my fourth child. I had an epiphany, sat up in bed and said, "I need to go back to grad school and study counseling." Because I was so outgoing, the connection with people fueled me. The feeling I had when I helped other people enriched and empowered me to give of myself in a way that was unique to me.

I could give them what is in me and I would be responsible only for that; what they did with it was up to them. I did not expect compliments or praise. Seeing the results is a benefit, but it did not fuel me. It was validating for me to feel the surge of energy come out of me and connect with them in a helpful way. After much research, I decided on marriage and family therapy, and it resonated with my core values.

Why does it take many people, me included, so long to realize our purpose in life? I believe a primary factor is that many of us are plagued with myths of what we hear and read about who and what we should be. This mindset is especially prevalent in minority community cultures. There are myths about what a "model" person a minority individual should be. These stereotypes especially affect Black, Asian and Latino individuals.

The model minority stereotype plagued me throughout my childhood without my realizing what it was. It was not openly discussed when I grew up. But, somehow, minority individuals learn about it sometime in our lives and have an aha moment that explains much of our distress. I really delved into the model minority stereotype in grad school for my therapy career, and it shed much light on my experiences. As I learned more about it through study and research, I became convinced of the role it played in my upbringing and believe it propelled me to the dark moment when I wanted to end my life at age fourteen.

Model minority stereotypes characterize a particular minority group as a monolith, all sharing the same identity. At the time of writing this book, we just finished a US presidential election where such monolithic stereotypes figured prominently in the print and TV news. Writers and pundits discussed, for instance, the "Latino vote," as though all Latino voters would vote for the same agenda. But the Latino voters in Florida did not think from the same perspectives as Latino voters in California or the Southwest.

Similarly, south Asians differ from southeast Asians and Pacific Islanders. The idea that everyone in a minority group fits a certain "model" is just a myth.

The model stereotype labels Asians in a monolithic manner. It labels us as being polite, law-abiding, quiet, and bowing our heads down. It includes the characteristic that we managed to obtain success through innate talent, despite being immigrants and all that entails. In other words, Asians set the standard for achieving high success. This is a myth; and stereotypes are not good, even if they include a "positive" characteristic. Today, more AAPIs (Asian American Pacific Islanders) speak out on the model minority because it is so embedded in our culture.

The model minority stereotype of Asians highlights the healthy and wealthy and masks our diverse community and disparities. While growing up, the stereotype placed me in a box of thinking "I am supposed to be perfect; and if I'm not, there is something wrong with me, and I don't fit in."

In my clinical practice, I try to dispel the myth of the model minority because it can cause people to view the ability to not feel or express their emotions openly as a strength. But it IS a strength.

I see the model minority stereotype mindset in many families today, and it places a tremendous burden on youth (like it did to me) to hold everything in and not share emotions because it is "not normal to do so." The stereotype says the person who shares emotions look pathetic, but Asians should be strong and do everything well.

From my perspective as a licensed mental health clinician, the model minority stereotype is detrimental and harmful to one's mental health and well-being. This term was first coined in the 1960s during the civil rights movement for Black Americans to gain equal rights in the US.

For Asians, the model minority stereotype's purpose was to put people of Asian origin in a collective group and pit us against one another, perpetuating systemic racism. Since I did not share the identity of the model minority of an Asian, I thought something was wrong with me. I thought my brain was different than the Asian brain. The reality: – indeed, it was.

The model minority myth allows no room for individuality or uniqueness of persons. Someone handed us something and we ran with it instead of appreciating the uniqueness that existed in each of us in academics, talents, personalities, complexions, and so on. A white sociologist who admired Japanese Americans back in the 1960s claimed the model citizens adjusted beautifully.

As I see it, the model minority myth is rooted in unhealthy origins and created a ripple effect over the years. This created such undue pressure and distress for Asians to live up to the model without realizing it.

For me, I was supposed to get perfect grades, and perfect scores on my tests and be the model student (meaning well behaved). It was almost like going against my DNA, feeling an emotion, but not giving myself permission to feel it.

Now, as a clinician, I do all I can to help people express their emotions, not judge them, and acknowledge that what they feel is what they feel. I always say that is important for a person's mental health to accept his or her emotions as they feel them. I am mainly concerned with what people do when feeling those emotions, making sure it does not result in unhealthy or unproductive behavioral coping patterns.

It is not easy changing something that so engrained for so long. I tell families that they can change history. Yet, I know they need more than that to be free. Some people struggle with their inner demons. But my demons were on the outside. They were in the voices that told me that I should be better or that I was not good enough.

My inner voice is where I find strength from my foundational faith. It is the voice that God gave me when I was fourteen. When I feel stressed, my inner voice chimes in to encourage me, reminding me of my strengths and why I am good. I choose to always listen to my inner voice.

My advice to clients and to readers of this book: You must give yourself permission to feel; discover who you are, not who someone says you are.

Sometimes I wish I could live in a bubble. I have a competitive drive from my Asian culture and am keenly aware of this. If I allow it to take over, I become toxic. Because I was always compared to others, I must stay grounded by practicing mindfulness.

Mindfulness is being grounded in the present moment, which is the only thing we can control. People who practice mindfulness are more apt to acknowledge their weaknesses and strengths. The practice of mindfulness must be focused and intentional. I work extremely hard at it; I practice what I preach. Sometimes we get so future focused, but we cannot control that. I tell people we can only control what I call the "what is" (the here and now). The "what is" for me is that I love what I do, and my parents stress me out. Mindfulness and being grounded in the present moment take practice, which I work on with myself and my clients each day.

So, back to my journey to discover my purpose. I can say with confidence today that I loved being a stay-at-home mom. All that I did then has come into fruition today. Now, in my therapy practice, I counsel many parents and lead parenting workshops, aside from other workshops I provide. Who my kids are today was the result of the time I spent with them at home. They received a lot of attention and nurturing, and that makes me happy.

My business school experience helped me be a savvier mental health clinician, running her own practice as an entrepreneur. I am validated in my purpose, and I see my upbringing as one of my strengths and a factor that made me the authentic, resilient woman I am today. I also use my broadcast skills as a national mental health speaker, calling people forward to change unhealthy patterns in their lives to promote good mental health and well-being.

It is exciting to finally behold who you are and realize that you are a person who has something to contribute to the greater world. The revelation of your purpose burns like a fire that cannot be consumed, to the extent that others feel the energy when you talk about it. That is where I am today and where I hope you will be after reading this book. I get excited when I talk about my purpose. And I am still curious about its full potential.

PART 2

Becoming the Leader of Yourself

Being a leader of yourself begins with understanding who you are. You will need to connect the dots to come to that understanding.

Our lives have seasons; and for each season, there is a purpose. In the early stages of discovering your purpose, it may seem challenging as to how it will all manifest. If you can stay on course, you will realize as I did how your story beautifully comes together and how nothing you experienced or did was in vain.

Chapter 4

Finding Your Purpose

C ulture and upbringing can be appreciated and valued without controlling you. To me, when people say they totally resent their culture or upbringing, it is as though they say they do not like themselves. Being a leader of yourself begins with understanding who you are. This must happen first. If you experienced trauma of any type, mental health is not a final thing; it is something you proactively work on consistently.

Admitting vulnerability is the first step. I am the first to admit that I struggle with perfectionism. But in the Asian culture, it is not acceptable to share one's struggles. However, to be healthy mentally, one must share their struggles.

You must be aware of what stresses you out. I cannot tell you how many times I ask that question to Asian clients who then readily admit that nothing stresses them out. I am much more intuitive than that, and I know that response is a defense mechanism. Being a leader takes courage. You must admit it if there is something depressing you.

In my practice, I ask open-ended questions so clients must answer something besides yes or no. I say what is considered bold things, but it gets their attention. Then we can have a conversation about what the problem is. I try to normalize the stigma of showing emotions while appreciating one's culture. People think it must be a case of "either or," but I make it clear that there is a parallel process where they can have something that they like for some reasons yet hate for other reasons.

I find that people want to hate their culture or part of their upbringing. I caution them to heal instead of hate. Hate only invites bitterness, which does not help anything. With introspection I feel you can understand what you think you hate. Healing can then begin with the focus on growth and love of self. I love to be introspective; it allows me to think through complexities and arrive at a reason that brings clarity for my growth. It involves acceptance and acknowledgement as well as interpreting situations for yourself. I will not tell you that this is easy. It requires maturity. When I was in my twenties, I did not think this way.

In college, I said that I was American and Korean; I accepted that I was both. When I became a mom, I had to accept being that too. Even now, I still work at forming my identity. I see a lot of stress in my field of work with youth struggling with their identity. I tell them it is a journey, and the outcome depends on their life experience and what pieces need to be worked through to arrive at a conclusion that they can accept and with which they can be satisfied.

Identity is never final. You constantly unfold and work on identity; it is a process. Until the day you die, you will try to figure things out about yourself in relation to your experiences. I always like to remind people of this: Put your oxygen mask on first. I share this advice all the time. It gives a person a chance to think first. Being a leader is loving yourself. And I feel that putting an oxygen mask on yourself first demonstrates that.

Your life journey is more than surviving the day-to-day routine; it is about sharing, learning, and growing. There are opportunities waiting for each of us that can stretch our minds a bit further to accept the possibilities that await us. But we must become familiar with our purpose and go through the process of maximizing our potential.

Years ago, I prayed about what I could pursue to be useful and make the most impact on the world. When I got the calling to be a mental health therapist, I took intentional steps to educate myself about all that it involved. As I toiled through that refining process, I realized how the things that I experienced earlier in life created a path and prepared me for my purpose today. I call it connecting the dots. I really had no clue what to do to find my purpose in life, so I did what I knew how to do: pray. When my purpose became clear, the refining process began. I had to look through broad lenses that allowed me to see everything, including where I was currently and how it connected with my purpose.

Earlier, I mentioned that my purpose literally came to my mind at 2:00 a.m. in the morning. I sat straight up in the bed with a jolt and said I was going to be a counselor, more specifically a marriage and family therapy counselor. Looking back over my life in retrospect, I see how the different experiences added to the becoming of my purpose.

It is more difficult to grasp how experiences come together when you try to understand and see it through young, inexperienced eyes. I like to think it is my responsibility to the generation after mine to share and hopefully lessen some of their anxiety about the unraveling of their purpose. I often tell college kids how I was super eager to get a job in my field of study when I graduated college; but now, twenty-five years later, I am doing something totally different. Your purpose can evolve. Your life and identity are a journey. Even today, I explore who I am as a mental health clinician.

It is important to keep in mind that our lives have seasons, and for each season, there is a purpose. I do my best to encourage young moms who are at home with their kids. Like me at one time, I could not see that my purpose when I was at home with my kids was a seasonal and legitimate purpose. I was in my early thirties when I had my fourth child. I told myself, "When he goes to preschool, I will get back to doing something purposeful in the work world." I did not know what it would be, but I knew it was not going to be journalism.

When we find contentment in the seasonal, purposeful periods of time, we can make new discoveries from engaging joyfully in what we do. When I learned this years ago, it sustained me. Your purpose at any given time depends on your current season of life. Whether you work at a career in your field of study or a have a nine-to-five job that you hold to bide time until your purpose is revealed, my hope is that you find some purpose wherever you are, even if it is just for a season.

Even when I had not yet understood my purpose, there was a form of refining happening in the background. When I went to business school, I focused more on how it would look on my resume than anything else; I wanted to look good on paper. But I did not like business school one bit. (I mentioned earlier in this book that I cried through business school.) Today, in my practice as an entrepreneur and owner of my own mental health practice, I use those skills I learned in business school. I never thought that I would end up in the mental health field. But unknown to me, my purpose was unfolding, becoming.

Counseling is what came to my mind in in the wee hours of the morning. My first thoughts on counseling were of working in marriage and family therapy. It seemed to be a comfortable fit. Even so, I researched it. People ask me how I got into counseling, especially marriage and family therapy. The simple answer is that my whole life prepared me for it. But the more complicated answer is that each piece of my life made its own contribution towards the sum of my purpose.

I then started researching that career. I wanted to know exactly what I was getting into as a career. I also spoke to other clinicians in the marriage and family therapy field and interviewed them. With four young children, I needed a school nearby. I was in Raleigh, North Carolina and found a marriage and family therapy program that was twenty minutes from my house. I would get the best of both worlds.

I also saw that one of the top schools was two hours away. Being the driven, competitive Korean that am, I considered going there, as that is how I was raised. I struggled with that for a moment, then shelved it. I feel I connect with marriage and family therapy because of the way I grew up. It held a power that I wanted to work with and share with others. Graduate school was therapeutic for me. Every time I learned something in class, I applied it in my life. What I experienced made sense to me, and I wanted to use what I learned to help others.

Recognizing your purpose in life involves a lot of self-reflection. Self-reflection is a process of viewing yourself honestly, noticing passions and patterns of what makes you feel good about your existence.

There are several ways one can engage in self-reflection. Meditation is one way. Prayer is another way. Whatever method of self-reflection you choose, the goal is to become more self-aware. I feel that graduate school prepared me for working in the mental health field as a clinician. The program forced self-reflection, pushing me to search for conflicts, bias, and unresolved issues within myself.

People sometimes ask me how I can listen to my clients' traumatic stories and separate from that once I get home. For me, listening to families about their traumas is easy. The moment I finish listening to trauma with one family, I can let go and move on the next family. This is not because I am callous but because I feel I have the strength to do so.

My sense of self is completely there with my clients during our time together. But the moment I leave and go home, I become a mom and a wife. I was really grounded in my family. People thought I would carry my work home and it would affect me in some way. I wear the badge of empathy proudly, maybe too proudly. But I know that becoming emotionally entangled with the trauma experiences of others to the extent of that influencing my life outside of the therapy room is not healthy. I learned how to separate the pieces of trauma from my life in handling the people I care for in my job.

When I decided to go into the mental health field, I was sure it was what I wanted to do. In my self-reflection process, I realized I wanted to understand the spectrum of metal health and mental illness and how to treat them. Sometimes treatment involves choosing the right medication because of the nature of the illness. To do that, I needed clinical experience.

Fellow Christians asked me why I did not choose to be a biblical counselor, since I am a Christian. My simple answer is that I am self-aware. But I know that does not explain it enough. Who I am as a Christian is something that is incorporated in everything that I do. When I care for my clients, they benefit from that. But they also benefit from my knowledge in helping their unique situation, which could mean being treated with clinical expertise necessary in providing psychoeducation surrounding mental health and mental illness. I believe biblical counseling is not enough, and I would not be able to help clients effectively because dealing with mental illness and mental health needs clinical training.

My process of self-reflection was helpful in getting me in touch with who I wanted to be in my profession and how I felt I could make the most impact. I encourage everyone to be familiar with where they fit to offer the best of themselves.

Through self-reflection, I realized how I could impact the Asian-American community in my work as a licensed therapist. I could do this by addressing mental health stigma and bring mental health to light in many aspects of the workplace in corporate life and in the community. To gain clarity, I had to push past the normal.

In my journey, I am open to the diversity that surrounds me. I do not run from challenges; it is a way to maintain learning. I press in further to investigate areas that seem unfamiliar to me. I met the unfamiliar when I was asked by a friend to do public speaking some years ago as a mental health clinician. I never planned for it or prepared for it. It happened. And I flourished at it. When things like that present as opportunities, it expands my purpose a bit more.

Through the process of self-reflection to recognize my purpose and refine it, I realized that what comes natural feels good. I advise you to keep in mind that it may feel a bit different working with your true desire at first, but it will feel more natural as you practice being your natural self.

The work involved in making the whole picture of your purpose come together becomes less confusing as you become increasingly aware of your unfolding purpose.

As you work on your goals, it is important that you remain faithful until the end and not give up on yourself. If you give up too soon, you will miss the opportunity to gain clarity that promotes growth and development with new ideas and abilities.

Making connections between how you were brought up and what your life purpose is will help you become your authentic self.

Chapter 5

Connecting the Dots

I mentioned at the beginning of Part 2 that becoming the leader of yourself involves connecting the dots of your life's experiences. Connecting the dots from one event to the next in my life allowed me to see a greater work taking place. In graduate school I learned a lot about theories as well as myself. I was amazed at how it all fed into whatever I did and provided the fuel I needed to keep going. Because of that, I could accomplish the next task. There was a constant connecting going on, and each event or situation trained me in a way that helped my bigger purpose.

I was a student of myself. I investigated my own identity and analyzed myself. I connected the dots from journalism to business school to being a stay-at-home mom to becoming a clinician. Even today, I still connect the dots as a parent. For twenty-five years, I witnessed the pieces of my life connect and move me to exactly where I need to be.

Even though I connected the dots, I still see in faded vision the Asian minority myth, and I remind myself that I will not be defined by that. When something is so engrained in a person's life, it is difficult to lose it completely. I still want to be the best; I still want to be perfect and prove that to my parents and family members.

To this day, perfectionism is still very much a part of my blood. It is one of my greatest strengths and what drives me to do well and work hard. But I also know its weakness because I constantly compete with myself. It is often referred to as "FOMO," the fear of missing out. I have that fear of not being acknowledged, accepted, and accomplished in society because I did not experience this while growing up.

It is constant work making connections with how I was brought up and then connecting that with my purpose and my authentic self and who I am today. I must listen to my inner voice.

Once, when a speaker introduced me, he connected me to what benefited him. For him, the fact that I am a trained mental health clinician and have kids qualified me in his mind and gave him assurance that I could offer something he could use. People can sometimes see and connect our dots for us.

I will now share with you some of the dots I connected, starting with giving and accepting support. Giving and accepting support was a foreign concept for me early in my life. I was not even familiar with asking for support. This was evidenced by the dark period I experienced with questioning my existence as I stood in front of that bathroom mirror years ago at the age of fourteen. I did not know how to ask my parents for help. In my culture, one did not do that.

I was a decent student; but when I really struggled at times, I could not reach out to the people in my life that I felt were supposed to be there for me. What held me back from asking for help, even many times before that dreadful moment, was a cultural piece engrained in my DNA: Do not ask for help; it is not the Asian way. We are supposed to excel and get straight As.

I was more than fortunate in my darkest moment to know enough about God and how He cares for us. Although God's love got me through that rough period, I still had something to learn. He helped me, but that did not mean other people would. I got to be forty-six years old and only asked my parents to help me only a handful of times. Whenever I asked for help, it always felt like I was in the "twilight zone." I remember clearly that I only asked when I felt it was important and concerned my kids.

There was a time when my husband had to have surgery, and he was laid up in bed. I was still in grad school, and we were raising four young kids. It was a stressful and vulnerable time for me. I had to attend classes that week and needed help with the kids. I remember saying, "Umma, Apba (mom, dad in Korean), can you come help me with the kids for about a week?" When their response was "no," I knew it was because it did not work with their schedule. I knew they would only say no because they were busy. But it still left me feeling bitter because the one time I asked for help, they could not help. So, I chose to miss classes that week to be home with my kids.

Since then, I learned to ask my peers for help. I went outside my cultural norms and reached out to my diverse group of friends. There was a time during the COVID-19 pandemic when I was down to only one can of Lysol sanitizing spray. I was in a panic because we are a family of six and we needed it. We looked for it in stores everywhere and could not find it. So, I sent a text message to my friends, asking them where to find Lysol. One friend responded that she was at Target and would pick up a can for me if they had it.

That baffled me. Here I am a mom (but not just that, a Korean competitive mom), who should have stored up the product. That experience may be common to others, but it broke down walls for me. Since then, I became better at accepting help from my friends. But not from my parents.

Obviously, I learned to give support to my clients. And I help people in my community. The COVID-19 pandemic and what everyone in our nation endures at the time of my writing this book is an example. Along with the protests and civil unrest, stress rose in the lives of many people. In my practice, I make a point to stay current on trends in online therapy and other forms of therapy that may be helpful. Constant research along with training and reading pertinent articles helps me embrace the knowledge of how I can better help my clients. I work to address mental health in all areas, the whole spectrum.

As I mentioned earlier, becoming is the unfolding of all that is in us on our way to our full potential. In the most stressful situations that we experience as individuals and as a nation, support becomes a necessary component. It pushes all of us to give.

Even if you do not have the same knowledge about God as I had that dark day when I was fourteen, God created you special. It is not an accident that you are here. Your life has meaning. Even if you do not know what it is yet, you can always start with giving and accepting support.

So, what connected the dots from my not being able to ask for help and support to my now helping and supporting others? The answer is the one constant in my life. What grounds me is my faith and my confidence in being a wife and mother.

In my own journey as a "tiger mom," I try to find balance so my kids will be happy, healthy, and balanced while working hard. It is a constant learning experience that requires strong faith! What I wanted as a child was emotional support and for my parents to not think I talked back all the time. Again, it was not good to talk back in the Korean culture, even if I intended to express myself and my feelings. Nonetheless, I wanted to be heard.

From a mental health standpoint, I find that people favor more emotional support. They can get logistical support from anywhere. They want validation, and they want to be heard. So, because of my experience growing up, I know to give that validation and support to my kids. Dots connected.

I have a relationship with my kids where I can ask them if they are stressed, and we can talk about it. I offer emotional support. At times, it makes me chuckle because, when I was growing up, that is not something that was offered to me. But that is what I work hard to give to my kids. I seek to be present and engaged with them. My parents were always busy. My dad was a busy doctor. My mom was a stay-at-home mom, but she did not engage with me. That was not something Korean parents did. It is time for a change.

My faith connects many dots. My faith is something I can depend on to remain constant in my life. It nurtures my inner being in a way that other things cannot.

I had the opportunity to work as an engagement leader for a group of Korean-American students and young professionals in an inaugural virtual summer program. In my introduction, I mentioned that one of my values is being a Christian. I did not think of it as something that stood out, nor did I remember it until a student inquired about it. Student after student visited me during my virtual office hours, stating how they identified with what I said. I loved hearing this from them because it made me realize the need they had in trying to put all the pieces of their young lives into something that would be meaningful. It was an opportunity for me to give.

The reality is everything changes. Every day we age. Our kids age too. We all experience new things. Even in my marriage, we are not happy one hundred percent of the time, nor is it normal to be. But we constantly grow and work on supporting each in good and bad times. What helps is we both share the same faith, so we align that way.

In my own personal journey, I remember going to Sunday School, and I hated it. But when my dark moment came about, I really recognized who God was. It went beyond what I learned in Sunday School. He saved me. Since then, my faith is a constant in my life.

In my work, I hear horrific stories of trauma. People ask me how I separate the traumas that I hear from my personal life. I answer, "It is my faith." I know it must sound strange to some, but it is true. My faith grounds me so that I can be one hundred percent attentive to my clients; yet, when I go home, I can switch to the role of mom and wife without being triggered by the things I heard at work.

I am not one of those people that carry their work home with them. And I do not feel that means I am less of a person because of it. I know that when I am at work, I give one hundred percent. When I get home, I want to give one hundred percent there as well. My faith allows me to feel secure in that way. My values help me separate all that. It is the underlying factor in all the decisions I make. I do not bring faith into every conversation. I do not feel there is a need to. During the pandemic, we had to adjust and now attend virtual church as a family. But we still pause on Sundays to acknowledge our faith. It is a time to nurture and give attention to what sustains us.

Some people think of Christians as radicals, and there are some that fit that description. Christians who I believe have not matured in their faith judge certain things and people harshly. The point that I make to encourage young people in the faith by explaining that everything they do is a choice.

I have self-control, and I love having fun. The two can co-exist. But I know that some people can judge doing certain things like drinking wine, dancing or listening to secular music. I encourage people to build their faith by reading their Bible and getting grounded in truth. My faith is constant in my life. I feel more equipped to do my job and live life because of my faith.

I connected a lot of dots in my life when I had children and became a "tiger mom." I wanted to intentionally parent my kids a different way than how I was raised. I saw that I could give to them and support them.

When I tell my children about the strictness of my parents while I grew up, they can hardly believe it. They quickly respond, "I don't believe you that Halmoni and Harabugi were ever that strict." But people who grew up with a tiger mom can relate.

When a tiger roars, it is heard. Tiger moms can be extreme. This type of parenting is different than the authoritative (balanced) parenting style. It is more about "all work and no play" and it is their way or the highway. There is no room to share or converse. Children should be able to share something with their parents. My mom talked at me, not with me. My life was incredibly stressful. Sometimes I would get spanked for playing the wrong piano note. But I was never scared of my mom.

The one I feared was my dad. People do not refer to tiger dads, but my dad was super strict even with being busy working. He was very disengaged, especially in my earlier years before high school. When he was in the house, it was scary for me because I did not know what my dad would say. It was like walking on eggshells. Every day when my dad would arrive at home, I literally hyperventilated and had an anxiety attack. He was not abusive; he just had a presence of sternness.

If you were to see my parents today you would not recognize them, based on what I describe from my childhood. I love who they are today with my kids. They spoil my kids and ask why I punish them. My kids can get away with what my parents considered talking back when I was young. Imagine what I think in those moments! Tiger parents do not tell their children that they love them. I knew they loved me because they were my parents. But the truth is I am happy that my kids get to experience a different version of my parents.

So, what connects the dots between the way I was parented when growing up and the way I now parent my kids?

My version of being a "tiger mom" includes choosing to enjoy life. I always plan fun things to do with my family, like berry picking and hiking. The kids sometimes complain, but I know later they will appreciate the memories. Those were not things I necessarily did while growing up. My dad would plan yearly family vacations, but I wanted weekly outings where I could get attention and spend a different kind of time with my family.

Though I am not exactly like my mother was, my kids at times think I am strict. I must admit there are some ways of mine that are like my mom. For instance, there were times they brought schoolwork home that had a grade of ninety-five percent. I would ask why they could not get a grade of one hundred. I am guilty of saying, "Try for a hundred next time. An A is good, but . . . ." I had to catch myself.

I am a tiger mom "2.0 version," which means being more emotionally in tune with my kids. I am not perfect. Sometimes, I must backtrack when I realize I sound like my mom. My husband is great about telling the kids that he loves them, but I struggle with that. I love my kids dearly, but I do not remember the last time I said it to them. I am learning that even though I show them that I love them in many ways, hearing the words is very important.

That leads me to my next important point: I am open for growth. This is a crucial mindset in becoming the leader of yourself. Life taught me a lot of lessons already, but I know there is still more to learn. I work to keep an open mind that is flexible and remain aware that I have a way to go.

It can seem like you are in a state of conflict with yourself when you do not approve of the ways you were parented. I have been there. I now feel OK sorting through the pieces of my life and holding on to the parts that benefit me and letting go of the pieces from which I cannot gain anything useful. I am proud of who I am. So, my parents did indeed do something right.

I tell young students who struggle with the same issue that hating their parents and trying to disengage from them is too extreme. You do not have to throw out everything because you do not agree with some part of it. There are some positives that come from our parents; culture is one of them. The things I like about myself and that you like about yourself, and the things we do not like about ourselves, stem from our upbringing. Think about it in terms of nature versus nurture: Asians are pre-wired fine culturally, but we could use some more nurture.

Hating myself is something I never did or said. As a tiger cub, I experienced extreme stress. Now, I am a tiger mom with four kids. My task is to find the balance for them that I feel. Some people try to do the total opposite by letting their kids do whatever they want. But I do not agree with that. I like that I had boundaries while growing up. And the strong work ethic that I now have is a quality my parents instilled in me. I guess I try to take the best of both worlds and find a way to instill that in my kids but include having fun.

I still have in my head the thought, "Why can't you just go to Harvard and get straight A's?" But I do not dare say that out loud. I manage it in my head because it was one of those things that I heard a lot while growing up.

I know I do not have to be my mom or dad. I can always create new pathways or choose what I want to take with me when moving forward. The same is true in your life.

It seems we always want what we do not have. It is best to accept the things that bring unity and authenticity to life.

Chapter 6

Culture and Core Values

P art of becoming the leader of yourself is learning to evolve beyond the early influences in your life and determining what to keep and what to throw away.

I had to learn to appreciate my Asian culture. I have not always done so. As a young girl experiencing pain, I did not know how to separate the useful pieces of my culture from the ones that were not as useful for my self-development. The Asian culture can be complex with all the different religions and practices it involves. The challenge is understanding one's uniqueness while dwelling in the vastness of the many practices of a culture.

I was born in Korea and came to the US when I was four months old. While I grew up, my parents took us to Seoul, Korea often enough. But I really and truly did not appreciate the experience because it was so foreign to me. I was used to being American and eating American food. Though I liked Korean food then and still do, American food was a staple in my life.

I begrudged my culture when we went to Korea. I would think, "Here we go again to Korea, and I must force myself to speak Korean." Speaking the language was not entirely the problem. My parents spoke Korean, so it was familiar to me. But I still resented it because I felt like such a foreigner. I related better to the American culture even though I did not look American.

It was probably right before my freshman year of college that I spent an entire summer at Yonsei University in Seoul, Korea. Like many other parents, my parents sent me there to learn the Korean language through a six-week language program. It was a program for Korean-American students like me. A lot of students traveled there during the summer.

It was draining, but I loved it. It was the best of the Korean culture I ever experienced up to that time. To experience it with other students that looked like me and struggled with speaking the language like me was comforting. I made some best friends there that I keep in touch with today, and that was 1992. Because of that experience, I started college with a good understanding of my Korean-American identity.

I recall when I was growing up how I just wanted to be like everyone around me in America. I was surrounded by a white culture; I grew up in a whitewashed neighborhood. A lot of my friends were white, and I had some Black friends too. I wanted to be whatever was not me. I did not like the way I looked, but going through the program in Seoul gave me a new appreciation for the Korean culture. I think maturity helped too; I had to grow up to appreciate it. Wisdom plays a role in things if we pay attention.

Then I started thinking that it was cool to be bicultural. I could speak both English and Korean. Some people have regrets about their past and how they did not embrace things sooner. That is not me. I am not the person that has any regrets about the process of how I got to this point of appreciation. I enjoy mixing the two cultures in my house today, the American and the Korean.

In fact, today, I love being Korean. It is funny to think that I resented it so much while growing up. I brag about it now. I think society changed since then. There are a lot more Asians today. We became a huge melting pot. The culture appears to be everywhere. There are plenty of Asian restaurants. In the 1970s and 1980s, we were not as visible. I see that my kids have a much easier time than I did.

Your culture is a huge part of your identity, even if you resent it. I tell people that it takes time to appreciate one's culture; it is something people do not understand quickly. It is a process. I share with my Asian clients my own quote: "Enduring the imperfections of our cultural heritage emboldens us to cultural confidence™; forging a path to impactful change for transformation."

Part of my resentment included the Tiger parenting in my upbringing. It seemed so strict and formal, like suffocating to the point of not being able to breathe. Another issue was I was jealous of my friends. I wondered what it was like to be white. I so wanted to have their blond hair. I recall how they would say they loved my black hair because it was so shiny. I think, "eww, stop saying that." My hair was straight and fine; their hair was curly.

Now, I try to maintain the originality of my hair. I appreciate my fine straight hair. It seems we always want what we do not have. But wisdom comes with aging.

Over time, I learned to accept the things that bring

unity to the culture. Things like family cohesion, responsibility, self-control, discipline, respect, and reverence for the elderly. Being direct is also part of the Asian core values. I choose to see the parts of my culture that are good and helped me become the person I am today.

Family cohesion and respect is such a big part of the Asian culture and a part that I had to grow up to understand. I remember growing up and not liking having to meet family members. Everything was about the family and showing respect. It was part of our ancestral culture that I just chose not to like at the time.

Even now, the whole elder respect situation can irritate me. For example, I can meet someone in my Korean culture, and if they are older than I am, it does not matter to me. But it is a big deal in the Korean culture. The older person would demand respect and feel like he or she knows more than I, all based on age.

In the American culture, I would consider someone in those age parameters my peers. In the American culture, I could be friends with someone ten years older than I and share mutual respect. But in the Asian culture, if they are older, it means they have more wisdom. This irritated me when I was younger; but now, I can laugh about it

The times when I did not conform to the Korean way, I got some not-so-good looks, or someone told me I was disrespectful. Being self-aware, confident, and choosing to make my own decisions is something I choose to do for my mental health. Sometimes, it shows up as not accepting everything that is thrown at me. I can decide what I will do at any given moment. In the Asian culture, I will get ridiculed and shamed in public if I show any disrespect to my elders. Bowing is a huge part of our culture; I do that today gladly out of respect of the Asian culture and to show I am proud of my identity.

There was an incident when I disrespected my maternal grandmother. When I look back on it today, I feel bad for my parents because I behaved as a brat. We were at the beach in Maryland, and all my extended family was there. This was the well-off, very educated side of the family. My grandmother told me it was time to eat, and I responded, "Oh, I'm not hungry," in my not-so-concerned voice. This triggered my aunt, my mom's older sister, to tell me that when your halmeoni tells you to eat, you eat, even if you are not hungry. I became irritated and mad. I fought it by saying it did not make sense, and I left the room.

Later, I heard from my younger sister that I embarrassed mom and dad, and everyone yelled at them. Image is important to Koreans, and I did not make my parents look good at all. Mainly my mom took the heat for my defiant behavior that day. This was around the time I was fifteen.

That incident was a turning point for me because, as much as I did not like the rules of the Korean culture, I did not like people yelling at my parents either. I decided to tolerate what I did not like. In retrospect, I say I exhibited that immature pride that teenagers have where they think they know it all. I could have just listened and sat there; my aunt even gave me that option. But I was angry. It was also a part of my showing what I did not like and trying to figure things out.

On a positive note, I used to feel that the discipline I received was suffocating; but, today, I feel it is probably the thing that made me successful. The hard work ethic my parents taught me allowed me to focus on my goals. Though I can take something positive away from that experience, there was a part that was extreme and not beneficial to my well-being. It is OK not to entertain the pieces of one's culture that bring more harm than good. In the Korean culture, there are several examples where people use shame for behavioral control. I consider that this, along with a few other things, should go into the throw-away pile.

Some things that stressed me out in my youth followed me into adulthood. Even with being the successful person I am today, because of how engrained the different cultural aspects were, I still must make a conscious effort to dismiss them. The need to prove myself, the shame and guilt I felt from not being perfect, and the emotions I could not show were more of a hinderance than anything else.

Not being allowed the space to show my emotions is probably the biggest issue I struggled with while growing up. Even today, I struggle with this as a mother. I struggle with saying "I love you" to my kids. Those words were not something I heard while growing up. I can say "I am sorry" and "I am proud of you" to my kids, though I did not hear those words while growing up. I think a child needs to hear "I love you." Just knowing and feeling it is not enough. Now, as a mom, I see that; yet it is a struggle and a big part of my vulnerability. Even at age forty-seven, I yearn to hear my parents say they are proud of me. I feel it is a huge part of feeling valued; so, it is something that I make sure I provide to my kids in my role as their parent.

Being in the mental health field does not mean that I somehow have everything figured out. Because of my upbringing, I work hard to have emotional peace; and I invite and nurture that as a mom. If my kids look stressed out or bothered by something, I make a point to talk to them about it, even asking them how I can help. My parents never asked me that. I have my own healing process and still do it to ensure that the emotionality is threaded out as I care for my family and nurture my kids. Those phrases that I did not hear growing up are so easily said in some cultures, but in the Asian culture they are uncommon.

I think people should pay some attention to why the suicide rate is high in Korea. I am sure it has something to do with being pressured on all sides by society and family. In the Korean culture, if you do not go to the top college, people consider you a failure. Koreans are known for being very direct, but not in a way that benefits people. Rather, they are a direct way to show where they feel someone's imperfections are so the individual can fix them and not misrepresent the culture. After all, we have an image to protect.

There were times when someone said something about my hair or said that I looked fat or looked too skinny, like a refugee. I was even told that I was stupid. There was a lot of shaming without considering the damage that could result.

Koreans do not think words hurt because emotions have nothing to do with it. They do whatever they can do to make someone do what needs to be done and not shame the family. If it means telling a girl she is ugly, then they will tell her that. Even today, comments boil down to a criticism; comments do not build towards growth and development. For that reason, I even limit my time on phone calls with my parents.

I tell my kids I know it is normal to get frustrated sometimes with other people in your family, but they need to use some self-control in how they handle that frustration.

Our annual family reunions were another example of added pressures that added to my stress and struggles while growing up. I felt the reunions were just a time for the moms to sit around and boast or brag about their kids. They viewed me as not achieving as much as my cousins.

It was a time to see which parent was doing a great job when it came to their kids' grades and accomplishments. Even though I was a good student, they did not view me as a good student because I did not get straight A's. I had cousins who got straight A's and were stellar students, even valedictorians. In American eyes, I was a good student; but in Asian eyes, not at all.

The funny thing is all of us cousins suffered in some way from that. None of us liked being compared to each other. Even the stellar ones did not like being boasted and bragged on at the others' expense. Now, my cousins and I can joke about it at times, but it was a trauma for me every year while growing up. I left the family reunions every year saying, "Yeah, I suck." A lot of what happened during those times culminated and led to the dark moment I had at age fourteen, standing in front of the bathroom mirror holding a handful of pills.

Even now, there is a lot of comparing of kids through Facebook posts things like what colleges the kids apply to or attend. Because of our American upbringing, we are a little more civil with it.

Again, I work hard at keeping my own mental health in check. And my kids' happiness is more important than what my family feels counts as success. I allowed my kids to choose the colleges where they felt they would be happy (with some guidance, of course). I work hard at making sure my kids know who they are and that they are happy with that.

PART 3

Your Authentic Reality and Success

When you have authenticity, you are grounded in self-awareness. You manage your feelings and responses to emotional triggers without sacrificing your true self. You do not change your core values to accommodate someone else's expectations.

Some people were brought up believing things are only either right or wrong. This can make it difficult when trying to keep what is beneficial for growth, especially when the right or wrong is according to someone else's beliefs.

Chapter 7

Manage Your Influences

We are exposed to many things that have the potential to influence us. These things come from how we were raised, friends, our environments, and other places. As we grow up, the task of sorting it all out may be stressful. Some of us were brought up believing things are only either right or wrong. This can make it difficult when trying to keep what is beneficial for growth, especially when the right or wrong is according to someone else's beliefs.

That is how it was for me while growing up. The strict Asian way seems straightforward. The right way is you get perfect grades, always behave, look good, and everyone thinks you are the best. The wrong way is if you do not do any of that.

When I treat someone's mental health, everything is gray. There is no black and white; black-and-white thinking is seen as somewhat unhealthy. That is technically not how our minds work. However, our minds go there, and there may be some conflicting stress with it.

I do not think things have changed much in the Asian culture since I was a little girl. I believe they still live life in black and white. I want to say it is getting better because of the younger generation and society shifting; but, overall, things are still black or white.

The last time I went to Korea was in 2012. Things were black and white then. In fact, if you walked into a room, you could tell who was American versus who was Korean simply by the way people were dressed. Americans believe when it is summer, they should wear shorts and T-shirts. Korean women wear decked-out dresses and believe it is the perfect way to present themselves.

While growing up, there was so much judgment. Everything was one way or the other. I sensed it even before words were spoken. This uses "noonchi," a key Korean skill that I will discuss more in my next book on parenting.

There was also a tendency to judge based on what is on paper. If a person went to Harvard or is a CEO, people think that person is very smart and important. It does not seem to matter if the person is sleazy or a terrible CEO. My struggle is from the Asian culture because it is not gray at all. I wish there were more fluidity.

I believe consumption plays a key role in relation to how we are influenced. We get to choose what we put in our bodies, minds, and those with whom we keep. As I become successful as a speaker, people want me to speak. I am learning to be more cautious, basically not letting people feed my ego. I think this is where my Christian faith comes in; I consider those who are humble to work with. I look at the way they approach me. I even look at the way they communicate through email. Even the humblest person can be super successful. So, I look at someone's humility.

Consuming is less physical for me than what I eat. Of course, I try to watch what I eat, but consumption has a lot to do with the people with whom I associate, including on social media. I am active on social media because I love keeping in touch with my friends and family and posting pictures. However, I do not go to other parts of people's pages to read their posts.

I believe social media comments about racism, politics, and things of that nature influence why threats and violence break out so terribly. There is quite a bit of bashing people on social media. For me, consuming that kind of influence would not be beneficial. Being in the field in which I work and people perceiving me as somebody who people go to for help, it can be tempting to offer an opinion that could help someone on hot topics. But I remain cautious and focused to not get caught up in these influences.

Resilience is imperative for success in life so we can learn and explore new perspectives when addressing the changes that happen in life.

Chapter 8

Build Your Resilience

Resilience enables people to respond to change or recover from trauma and disruption. Building resilience is not automatic. It is a process of exposure to disappointments and pain while figuring out a way to accept it but not allowing it to deter you from living in your purpose. You can learn and develop resilience.

Gaining wisdom and having a good sense of self-awareness is key to building resilience. Although events in our life cause us pain, it is imperative that we explore new perspectives because life happens despite the situations we face. Adopting healthy coping mechanisms and accepting the challenge of learning and developing wisdom sets us on the path to resilience.

Being authentic requires resilience. My definition of resilience shifted over the years. Prior to becoming a licensed mental health therapist, I thought resilience did not apply to me. I thought, "Oh, this is just for the special people who went through a difficult trauma." I did not try to downplay my experience; I just thought it had to be for people who literally suffered a near-death experience or went through a lot of tragedies.

As I went through graduate school, resilience came up a lot. That is when I began to understand it more. The definition of resilience seemed to go beyond what could be explained in words. I remember thinking in graduate school that I completely misunderstood resilience. I started realizing that resilience applies to me. I realized everyone develops their own resilience journey. In this book, I share my journey.

So, I now realize that everyone has resilience. It is the core of my solution-focused model of therapy (which I cannot take credit for). It is an evidence-based model that is a family therapy practice that I really value. This is the model I adhere to in a lot of the work I do. The core of it is everyone has their own resilience. It can look different because everybody is unique.

I love the word resilience. It exudes like a feeling more than a definition of strength. It is almost like an emotion that comes out. Now, it is a big part of my job; and I kind of laugh about it to show people they are resilient. That is what my work is about.

Change must come from a person's own journey. I remind those who come to me for therapy that their resilience does not come from me, but from them. When I say that, it seems like an impairment and seems kind of frightening to them. I go on to explain how people must build resilience over time and in fact is there already. We do not see it because, when things happen, we do not always focus on how strong we are. It is more common to focus on how bad we feel or what we did wrong.

But, in time, we can become aware of our resilience if we take time for introspection and examine our lives in more detail. I tell people to take care of their resilience when things are good. That way, they have something to stabilize them in the challenging times.

Fear influences our thinking of what is right or wrong. Fear is multi-dimensional; it comes in many different forms. Fear brings a lot of anxiety. But denying fear perpetuates it.

Chapter 9

Manage Your Fears

Fears cause us to react to life in varied ways. The most therapeutic response to fear is to admit that you have it; only then can you strategize how to deal with it.

Some will say that fear is not real. I disagree. Fear is real. We experience it like any other emotion. I do not recommend you feed fear, but the truth is someone's reality is their reality. This is a mental health concept. Fear is an emotion like sadness, or joy. In that way, it is a part of life.

Christian faith speaks of fear in several ways. It talks about fearing God as a way of honoring His position. It also talks about fear as something to take to God in prayer, as He can provide comfort to us from fear.

So, fear does exist. Denying fear perpetuates it. I associate fear a lot with anxiety. Anxiety comes from what we are fearful about, and a lot of it is normal. A good example is people feeling fearful of catching the coronavirus during the pandemic. This brings about anxiety, but it is completely normal. I put on my mask, wash my hands, and use hand sanitizer because it is something I can do to be cautious and it makes me less likely to get the coronavirus.

Obviously, it is not healthy to live in a continuous fearful state. You should not feed fear, as it will increase and becomes bigger. Then like a virus, fear literally infiltrates a body just like a cold, with the ability to make one contagious and spread the fear to others. That is an unhealthy way to live.

When someone says to me, "I am really scared of this" or "My fear is this," I allow the person to use those words. Again, someone's fear is a part of that person's reality. But my reality is completely different. Our realities can be different. Downplaying or saying someone's fear is not real can make that person feel insignificant and invalidated.

My job as a licensed mental health therapist is to make sure my clients manage their fear as best as they can. So, I acknowledge it and encourage my clients to use words to describe their fear. Then we can understand the problem and outline solutions.

I guarantee you, living in fear is not helpful to you or those close to you. Fear can affect every area of your life. I like to think of it as managing anxiety. I do not say, "How do we get rid of it?" To say that is almost like saying, "How do I stop breathing?" Just like your emotions are part of your life and need to be managed, fear is the same way. This is where my skills come in, helping people to be familiar with their own fears and validate them. A lot of us have the same fears. And fear is totally real.

Asians deny fear. Yet, I feel the fear of failure drives Asians. My fear did not come from my parents. Fear is one of those emotions that were taboo; yet it drives actions and behaviors. The Asian community ends up showing fear to be the forefront emotion, mainly by the meaning they associate with it. The fear of failure may be the biggest association. Then there is the fear of looking bad and the fear of imperfection, and I am sure there are more.

In my own upbringing, I do not think I sensed a lot of fear in my parents. I did not grow up feeling particularly good, as I was afraid of not looking perfect and made sure I followed all the rules. I am sure that I developed some fear just from the expectations. So, my fear during my upbringing came from myself. I believe that is how it manifests. You cannot blame somebody else for your fear. Right? But growing up, I blamed my parents for it.

I now identify with being solution-focused as a model to help people shift their perspective. Through the practice of mindfulness, brain retraining (neuroplasticity) can happen, but it takes a lot of work. People must believe in their own resilience. The fear that I had while growing up was the fear of not being good enough, hence, the episode at age fourteen. I thought, "I am probably going to fail them; so, I might as well just take my own life."

I am thankful that I do not have that fear today. Aside from the typical worries of my kids and family, I came to terms with where I am today. I do my best to practice what I preach. Every day in my work, I talk about mental health and talk about emotions. It is a constant reminder of where I should be and probably saves me.

After much reflection on my past fears, I realize that my fear of not living up to preset expectations of my culture was completely something I allowed myself to feel. I believe my stressful upbringing exacerbated those feelings.

Replacing fear with a different focus, like your purpose, impacts the world around you. It demonstrates your understanding that your existence is purposeful. The reality is you will have problems, but you still have a bigger reason to be here. This leads the way into creating solutions.

The solution-focused model is evidence-based. It was co-founded by a Korean-American woman who is no longer living. It is a newer model of therapy. I learned of this model in graduate school and decided to embrace it. It is the core of my work, which I think makes any nurse, doctor, or therapist, or at least doing well in their practice, if they believe in what they are doing. With this model, we do not look at the problems. We look at the solution to the problems. It is human nature to look at the problem. It is easy to point out every problem under the sun. There could be one solution, and everybody would ignore it. This is where I put in the work: finding exceptions to the problem.

A good example is when I ask clients when they do not feel fear, and they say something like "When I play the piano." They do not feel like this is a big deal, but I see a solution in that. If you are afraid, the solution is to manage the fear. If playing the piano offers calmness and peace, the person should do routinely, not sporadically. Maybe it means to become a concert pianist. If the person could imagine playing a beautiful note on the piano, he or she could perhaps alleviate fears in that moment.

I help people with their fears; I do not take fears away completely. I am even careful about using the word "overcoming" in relation to fears. I believe you can overcome a fear of heights if that makes sense. Physical fears you can overcome. But I do not think overcoming the emotion of fear itself is possible. We do not overcome our debilitating emotions; we manage them so that we do not let them control us. This is not rocket science; but in the field of mental health, language is immensely powerful. So, how I use my words is important so that my clients understand.

Success comes in many forms. But only you can define what success is for you. This means you have control of the steps that you will take to obtain it. Living your best life possible requires that you be whole, which may require constant monitoring of your mental health. Healing must happen in a holistic manner, working from the inside out, giving your best to yourself, forgiving yourself and others, and living a life of gratitude.

For me, success is my making an impact. An impact could be influencing change in someone's life. It could also involve impacting the life of my kids. I get to choose what the success is. My meaning of success was rooted in my Korean upbringing.

The Korean culture relates success to the highest level of education achievement, marrying a doctor, or performing at the highest level in a prestigious musical opportunity. I remember a non-Asian friend saw me as successful because of my having my four kids and husband (that was before I had my mental health practice). That was success to her.

At that time, I looked at success through the lens of workplace and career. Since then, my perspective changed. I now connect success with being happy. I am happy about what I do.

I am not saying you should or will be happy every day. Sometimes you may feel stressed. But the takeaway is success should be something you feel happy about. There are people who seem to have it all as far as money and material things go, but do not feel happy or successful.

In my work, I help people work through forgiveness and healing. All of this is rooted in my faith. Again, healing and forgiveness are a journey and are cyclical. I am still healing today; and I know it because I can still get triggered. Putting in work on your own healing process is being responsible to those you care for. It gives them the best of you.

I think it is worth mentioning that people can fear success. When we build resilience and finally get to the place where we are successful in what we do and people seek us out because of that success, we can get cold feet. I can relate to this feeling. I call it the fear of success. It is the feeling that people will expect something of you when you are successful. That feeling may create a fear of not being able to measure up to people's expectations, or it may create pressure bringing on stress.

Although you may be successful, when success makes you feel anything other than happy, you need to manage those feelings. For example, I encounter the imposter syndrome. It happens at times when I am about to speak or lead a workshop. It is for a coveted audience and great for my career, and I am proud to have the opportunity. However, in the moment of feeling the imposter syndrome, I consider that the audience might like me, which could lead to more opportunities; and that would mean more work for me to do. So, I go in the opposite direction.

In closing this chapter, I want to give you three tips to help build your resilience even more. Again, success is how you define it. We are unique individuals, but I believe the following points are fitting for wherever you are in your journey.

Keys to Success

- Build on your strengths. Success is not about working on your weaknesses. Just manage the weaknesses. But hone, emphasize, and build on the strengths you have. That is what will make you successful and happy. Why not exploit your strengths?

- Seek out solutions when you are not stressed or feel pressured. Think of things that challenge you the most and that cause you to be fearful. Then find a time when you are not in a state of fear and your resilience comes out and you are confident. Practice feeling that way all the time. It will bring about success because of what you exhibit of yourself.

- Prioritize your relationships. Everything boils down to how happy you are in your relationships. We do not live in a bubble alone; relationships are all around us. Your task is to prioritize the quality relationships that make you happy and are nurturing. In the end, that is what will sustain you. You will retire from your work one day, but your relationships will still be there. The regret I hear the most is not having spent more time with family or friends.

How much input and effort does it take to be impactful? This is something we all ponder as we search for a balance between work and family life and even life in general. Being impactful requires authenticity and being mindful to stay balanced.

Chapter 10

Impact Your Workplace

As an Asian American, I saw where I could be impactful in my work as a mental health clinician. It allowed
me to reach other Asian Americans because I could
relate to their needs. My personal research data and work
added insight to how I engage and the skills I use to make an
impact with Asian-American families, students, and professionals.

I did not plan to have the career in mental health that I
have today. I feel it is a pleasant blessing for me to do what
I do. I think of that little girl who planned on being the
number-one famous journalist and lived among a family of
doctors. Never did I plan on working in the field of mental
health. I also remember being a stay-at-home, full-time
mom, waking up in a fog and not knowing what day it was.
My life was so different then. I never expected to be a solo

entrepreneur running my own business, doing speaking engagements, and making my own impact.

You can plan all you want to, but life happens. Life's circumstances can change. I could not have predicted where I am today. We just do not know the future. I tell my clients that being so set on something happening can cause stress and anxiety because life can change.

Working in mental health was not on my radar, mainly because it is very stigmatized in the Asian community and culture. Many Asian parents will not talk about mental health, let alone say that they want their child to work in this field. The taboo or stigma still exists. Of course, being a doctor, lawyer, or engineer is very mainstream. I am proud to say I enjoy being a trailblazer because I address the mental health stigma, and that is my passion. In the Asian-American community, whether it is cultural or college, or in families or in the corporate American workplace, the social stigma surrounding mental health is very much a reality.

When I raised my kids, the thought of going back to work full-time felt foreign. Especially considering all the hours I now work. It makes a difference now that my kids are older. Timing and your current season of life plays a role. Impacting the workplace today can happen even when you take time off. Sometimes moms may feel like they cannot take time off, and that can bring feelings of guilt. The guilt is very understandable.

There should be some balance between giving something to the workplace and being there for your children and family. For my own sanity, I chose to be a full-time mom while I was in graduate school. It was a good choice for me because I knew my work ethic could lean more towards being a workaholic, partly because of my personality and partly because my Asian upbringing. I could not handle both raising young kids and working full-time and building my career. So, I know an impact can happen later in life. The takeaway is to be mindful of every moment and appreciate it—because things change.

When considering how to be impactful in my work, I knew I did not want to just go to work and give my clients something that would just get them by. I wanted them to leave feeling like we met a core need.

I had an experience earlier when my own passions were not addressed. This caused me to self-reflect and re-examine my intentions and goals.

In that experience, I took a job that placed me at my lowest emotionally. If I had to diagnose myself, I would probably say I had situational depression. I accepted a job that was very toxic. I made the choice willingly because I wanted to look good. This is where the Asian culture and my upbringing clashed with the woman I had become two or three years before accepting that position. I ignored the red flags.

I was already a licensed clinician, but I put my passion on the back burner to fulfill a role that involved my leading a women's empowerment organization. I believe my being a clinician and Asian American appealed to the CEO. I took on the position of COO. I lasted fourteen months. The idea that the position would make me look good and allow me to be the best I could be, and I could tell people that I was the COO, is what drove me. Ironically, taking the job caused my mental health to take a huge hit.

I knew I was suffering from situational depression, a type of adjustment disorder, because I diagnosed a client with the same condition. I kept my private practice on the side. While taking notes as the client told me about his workplace, it hit me: Everything he described related to what I was going through in the COO position.

The thing about depression is it does not look like what you think. People think that walking around looking morose, gloomy, or constantly crying is what depression looks like. They are right; it can, indeed, look like that. But a lot of the depression I see, especially for people in the workplace, manifests as extreme irritability, frustration, and a negative, pessimistic outlook. That was me, and I did not recognize myself. I could not leave the job right away; so, I depended on my faith and prayer to get me through that situation.

Putting your passion on the sideline while you build a resume that looks good on paper is not worth your trouble or time. I put aside my passion and all the work I did in graduate school to just look good. Therefore, I am effective today when I treat corporate clients because I know what it is like to want to climb the corporate ladder.

In that job, I learned a lot about workplace abuse (not to be confused with sexual harassment). I never tried to threaten the CEO with my self-confidence; I feel the abuse was more a case of my being confident in my skills and standing out as an Asian-American female leader.

I envisioned using my therapy skills of being a communicator and being able to empathize and build people up. I thought I would make a huge impact in the organization, practically leading the organization because I was COO. It was a global organization, and I wanted to impact women around the world. The passion and mission of that organization that was on paper drove me.

But you never know how toxic a situation is until you are in it. It does not matter what the organization's name is or what its mission states. I ended up not making any impact while on that job. I was not allowed to do any of the things I was good at: rallying people and inspiring them, mentoring, managing, and speaking.

One way of making an impact in the workplace is building connections. You cannot build connections without knowing people and what they need. Because I am an Asian American caring for Asian Americans in my mental health work, I could relate to the issues they had and connect them to the proper help or service.

The irony is, while growing up, I did not want anything to do with Asian Americans. This is mainly because I did not have a good impression of them. Then, when I was in graduate school, I had the idea that maybe being a second-generation Korean American could be useful in building a connection with Asians and my Korean-American community.

The connection I made was right before I became a practicing clinician. I could relate with some of the things they went through. I was a parent. I was also raising kids about the same age as some of the people with whom I connected. I understood being the child of immigrant parents. For the younger generation who struggled with identity, I was familiar with that as well.

The connections I make today result from my upbringing. It is as if my experiences growing up with all the challenges I faced were a bridge that led me to where I am today. I do not view those times as terrible as I did at one time. I can see now how they prepared me for my purpose. I want to make this clear: I disliked my upbringing so much that I never imagined I would be grateful for it. But I am very grateful because it allowed me to help the people I serve today.

The resilience I experience today as a therapist comes from my learning and coping during those challenging times. I think my credibility comes across when a fellow Asian American sees another Asian American to whom they can relate and can share their story. The mental health field is not remarkably diverse. I want to see more Asians as well as other cultures reach this population where mental health is stigmatized and psychoeducation is very much needed.

Your experience is your training ground that leads you to your bigger purpose in life. A lot of times it is hard to be aware of this in the moment of challenges. But if you challenge yourself to grow, you will realize how connections build from experiences to those with whom you engage in your work.

To make an impact in any endeavor (or do anything well, for that matter), requires your inputting time, effort, and understanding. At a young age, my parents ingrained in me the need to be the best at whatever I did. During my journey to where I am today, I did not lose that focus. My work ethic always involves putting in time learning and discovering with the goal of acquiring the best understanding of whatever it is I do. I spend time doing my own research, which adds insight to the work I do.

Exploitation is an issue you must consider when you try to make an impact in the workplace. When I first started working in the mental health field, it was in primary care medicine. I worked with doctors and found it fitting because I grew up in a family of doctors. So, the medical language was familiar to me. However, I struggled with some issues. I always thought of myself as an outlier, which is how I feel I got to where I am today. I never was that typical good Korean-American kid. I questioned things much of the time when I felt they did not make sense.

In this role in primary care medicine, I was the top therapy provider in the organization. I was proud of that, and I brought in a lot of revenue. But I fought constantly to not be exploited.

I wanted recognition. I felt that if I put in the hard work, I should at least be recognized for it. In this position, I wanted to be seventy percent therapy provider and thirty percent business leader. I was their first therapist hire, and I knew they respected what I brought to the organization.

I fought against a bunch of men, and the organization ended up giving the role to a man. To their credit, the man was ten years older than I. My frustration came from the fact that I had a business degree. This experience made me even more motivated to be a trailblazer in the field of mental health. In moments like these, it is important to drum up your courage and make the best decision for you.

Believe me when I tell you that I am familiar with some of the snags that you will face as you put in time and effort to make your impact. As an innovative, outspoken, and professional entrepreneur and Korean-American woman, I get my share of stereotypical questions and stares. Even though this disappoints me, I do not allow it to detour me from my vision of making an impact in the field of mental health.

I must continue to be a leader in whatever space I am in. And I am proud to lead the way in mental health. So, I use bold statements that can sometimes be shocking to hear. As a therapist, I can ask those questions that may not seem appropriate in another situation. Sometimes, people think leadership is looking perfect. But I think leadership is about being bold and courageous, but mostly introspective. Be aware of who you are; then you can ask others to do the same.

So, how much input does it take to be impactful? I think this is something that we all ponder as we search for a balance between work and family or in life in general. I learned how to input all my strengths to do what I do. And what I do grew over time as opportunities came to me.

You never will know what you can do unless you explore some opportunities. Along with that, you also must be comfortable with saying "no" and not accepting every opportunity. This relates back to being self-aware and monitoring your own mental health.

The most important thing for me was to be authentic to myself while making sure I was there for my family and using them as support. If things were good with my family, I could make the biggest impact in my work. My practice of mindfulness and focus on my Christian faith allows me to stay balanced and true to my family and those I serve in the mental health field.

In closing this chapter about challenges in being impactful, I want to add some thoughts about the COVID-19 pandemic we all face (at the time of this writing). The pandemic presents a challenge to being impactful as well as finding support and balance. The isolation and distancing rules, it can be difficult for even the most optimistic person who will Zoom or connect in other ways with friends and family. Even so, the task is to be intentional by scheduling time to enjoy those you are with and enjoy time with friends. I feel this presents the best outcome of being impactful in your current space during a historic pandemic.

Feeling lonely, isolated, and disconnected are real feelings that could be the trigger that precipitates mental health issues in some vulnerable populations. Making an impact is something we all probably do on some level every day in our workspace and home life. My hope is that even the pandemic encourages you to continue making an impact while also expanding your reach. My life teaches me that there is so much more in us that we can do when we are confident in strength and when we input effort.

You must learn to balance who you are becoming and must incorporate the yin and yang in your life.

Chapter 11

Balance Your Inner Tiger

In the previous chapters, I shared how my life evolved from the time I was a young girl. I am far from the end of all that I have left to experience, learn, and explore in this life. My journey continues as I continue to be more self-aware.

In this chapter, I share with you how I intentionally balance my inner tiger. If you read this far in the book, you know I do not throw away anything from my past. The person I am today is the result of all I experienced. I had high expectations for myself that made me push hard to achieve my goals. I had to learn balance, how to incorporate the yin and the yang in my life. I knew I needed both, but in a way that would benefit me instead of harming me.

I find it quite interesting that I was born in the Year of the Tiger. Koreans tend to follow the Chinese zodiac of the lunar calendar. The Tiger zodiac sign represents a brave, competitive, unpredictable, and confident personality. Tigers can also be stubborn. Things like this make for good conversation; but speaking from my experience while growing up, I was not allowed to express whatever brave or confident personality traits I had.

Of my tiger parents, my mom was more of the disciplinarian, the "bad cop." My dad was at times a worst cop; the stoic, silent type. I could not quite read him. Quietness is a big thing in the Asian culture. My mom was loud and brash, as well as a yeller. I preferred that. It was harder for me walking on eggshells, wondering if my dad was going to scrutinize me that day. I think I held my breath most of my childhood. My dad had a silent roar, almost like a low growl; and those roars can be tougher. My mom had a loud roar that I learned to deal with. It was intense at times.

In my youth, I knew little about balance. I knew I liked to play, but I did not get to play much. I am an extrovert and enjoy being around people. But I was not always able to exercise being an extrovert. My personality was always outgoing. But I had to be cautious of what I said, as my environment was not conducive to dialogue. It was monolog, parents telling me what to do and talking at me and expecting me to listen.

Even with this happening, I do not believe my childhood was unhappy; but it was extremely tense and anxious. My mom would hit my hand with a wooden spoon if I played an incorrect piano note. However, as time passed, I appreciated the discipline. I managed to find my own identity through that and use it to my benefit.

But there was still the work of balancing all of who I was as a child with the woman I was evolving into. I had the best of both worlds. I just needed to understand how they could coexist to enrich my life and others' lives.

There is an ancient Asian philosophy called "Eum-Yang," better known as "Yin-Yang" in Chinese that people believe has the purpose of creating balance when engaged properly. In Korean culture, the symbol of yin and yang is represented in the Korean national flag called "Taeguk." Perfect harmony and peace are said to be the result when there is balance of the yin and yang. I cannot say that I knew what balance was growing up, let alone how to achieve it through yin and yang or eum-yang. But as I grew up, I defined it myself. Growing up in my Korean home, there really was no balance; it was all one way. The Korean way.

Without going too far into the origin of yin and yang, I think it is important to define briefly what each part represents and how I came to understand it as it relates to my growth and health. Different literature seems to agree the yin is the negative force and yang the positive. Yin is believed to be the universal force that is not seen nor can be touched. Yang is believed to flourish and grow because of the yin. There are so many ways to think of this. I like to think of it as who I was before marriage and who I am after. Because of the contrasting versions of me, when it comes to self-improvement, I view it as competing with myself.

My yin was Jeanie Bae. I experienced conflict because of my interpretation of her upbringing. It caused me to focus on the negatives, which Jeanie Bae could not express. It caused internal struggle and conflict. I rejected my culture and upbringing. I tell my clients to do this is not productive to mental health. I find that people struggle when they want to reject it.

My yang is Jeanie Chang. She is much wiser and more balanced. I work extremely hard to find that balance. That is why I chose to give up my journalism life years ago or else I would not have a family today. I would be unhappy. I had to make harsh decisions to balance things. My yang flourishes because of my yin.

We need both the yin and yang to be balanced; One should not overtake the other; one defines the other.

Another element that I feel adds something to the yin and yang is the term "dialectics." Used in mental health, it is having two different factors or polar opposites happening at the same time. An example is that you can love your parents but not want to deal with them. Nothing is black and white. It is a constant awareness. You do not need to throw out anything, as two things can exist at the same time. You can investigate and discuss them in a way that unveils knowledge for your better understanding.

I mentioned earlier that I now think of myself as Tiger Mom 2.0. When I became a mom, I did not want to raise my kids like my parents raised me. It remains a concern throughout my journey today since I show tendencies at times to put intense pressure on my kids and expect a lot of them. Not only was I tiger parented, but I was also judged by my extended family. I provide for my kids a healthier version of what I grew up with, which includes aspects of my culture that I still identify with now, and finally, appreciate.

The definition of Tiger Mom 2.0 came from a colleague who called me that term when I attended therapy graduate school. He meant it fondly, and I adopted that term ever since because it fits me. I call it resisting the roar. Because of my upbringing, I add that it is being able to provide emotional safety for my kids. If they want to express openly when they are overwhelmed, I allow it. I intentionally never tell my kids that they should not be stressed or feel what they feel.

It is the trendier version of tiger parenting. The 2.0 is for the second-generation Korean American, which I am. I have seen some Asian moms be taken aback when they hear the term Tiger Mom 2.0. I am OK with that; it is my interpretation.

Balancing push and pull also is important. I wanted to be sure that when I pushed my kids to achieve that I also pulled them in closer to me. I feel it is important to show them love in the way they recognized and needed it. This can be different for each child and requires asking or observing what they respond to. The push was much easier for me because that is what I saw growing up. The pull is more challenging for me.

When my kids were younger, nurturing them verbally with the words "I love you" seemed natural for me to say. As they grew older, it was tougher for me to do that. I can do the nonverbal of the pull. None of this is the result of a lack of love of any sort; I believe it is the result of what was not modeled for me while growing up. My challenge since that time is to work at balancing my inner tiger, but it did not come easy at those times. I must train my brain to say nurturing things. I did not have that push--pull model throughout my childhood.

Growing up, I was considered the "black sheep" among my cousins. I remember saying that I would not have kids when I grew up. So, when I was the first one to have kids (four at that), it surprised everyone. All eyes were on me then to see how I would parent. There were questions like "What kind of grades do Jeanie's kids make?" or "What Ivy League schools will they apply to or go to?" Family members judged and contributed pressure to my parenting style. I was triggered when I got the speech from my parents making sure our kids went to the top colleges. It was the tiger parent coming out in the form of Tiger grandparents.

Before pushing yourself in any direction, you must first discover your core needs.

Chapter 12

Address Your Core Needs

I t is not always easy to identify your core needs, especially if you are not self-aware of what motivates or drives you to make decisions. Awareness of your core needs can make you more intentional in finding ways to meet your needs.

Your core needs can change depending on your stage of life, but your core values do not change. Psychologically, as a child, I needed more play time, affirmation, and affection. But as a teen, I wanted independence and wanted to be left alone; I was a typical teen. At the time, I was not thinking about core needs nor could I probably identify them if asked. Because of the clarity and self-reflection processing I did as an adult, I now can identify what I feel is the common theme for me: I wanted to be able to openly express my emotions. Of course, that was not offered.

I recall intentionally trying not to show that I was stressed out while growing up. This happened especially when I had piano performances. They were extremely stressful, and I could not tell my parents how I felt. I had a lot of stomachaches, especially before recitals. Sometimes I had dry heaves. I now know that was due to the anxiety and pressure I felt. I believe expressing my feelings to my parents in those times would have alleviated my anxiety in a way that was healthy to manage and I would not have felt so alone in my turmoil. I also remember experiencing a stomachache right before I grabbed those pills when I was fourteen during the darkest moment of my life.

When you hold back an emotion to where you cannot define what you feel, your mental health really takes a hit. I emphasize this repeatedly to my clients. The first thing I think you should be able to do as a child is experience psychological safety in your home, that is, be able to be yourself and feel comfortable showing your feelings and true self without fear of any consequences. Even if you do not express your emotions, just believing that you feel you are in a safe space to do so can be enough. I do not recall feeling this way while growing up in my own home. Again, I want to be clear that I felt loved, just never really at ease or at peace. This is taxing on any child or adolescent.

When my clients share that they should not feel a certain emotion or question why they feel what they feel, I begin by indicating that it is normal and perfectly OK to feel whatever emotion they feel. That is how they feel!

I tell clients my main concern is what unhealthy behaviors or thoughts come out of those emotions that could result in adverse effects (for example, throwing something at a person out of anger or self-harming due to anxiety and distress). I do not tell clients that their emotions are wrong or do not make sense. This would be invalidating. However, it is rooted as a cultural norm in the Asian community; especially when showing vulnerability by crying.

Another example is when little boys cry; Asian parents tend to tell them it is not right for boys to cry. Yes, this still happens today. A common emotion expressed In the Asian culture is anger. Again, this is another aspect of our culture, but people do not express it in a healthy manner. In fact, I find in my work that I must reserve the troublesome effects that Asian anger holds in the family.

Becoming your authentic self and enjoying success in what you do involves introspection and change. Making sure you have some wiggle room as you change is critical to success. This is why I call my private practice "Your Change Provider." I want to provide impactful change, and that is my solution. As you evolve through change, allow yourself some room to grow and make mistakes. This is not easy for me to admit. Sometimes, you can make things too rigid when trying to do things perfectly and create too much pressure on yourself.

Being authentic involves understanding your own narrative, which helps make sense of your reality. As far as I could see when understanding my true self, I had three things to work with: my tiger parenting, my Korean culture, and my inherited perfectionism. From my dad's side of the family comes a super-critical, overly perfectionistic gene. I see those tendencies in myself every day.

I am OK with making mistakes in certain things, but I struggle with making mistakes when it comes to my work. This is important, and I can admit this: I like to make sure I look good in front of my fellow Korean Americans. In the Asian culture, what you do and how accomplished you are defines you. Even today, I struggle with this all the time.

This stems from my experience of the Korean culture in my upbringing. The fact that I had to constantly prove myself growing up as well as not feeling that I was good enough is a result of the pressure I often feel today.

I do not want to totally fault the Korean culture, though it was exhausting. It is also probably why it took me so long to get to where I am today because of trying to look good by doing the career paths I chose. Koreans are my biggest critics; so, when it comes to anything to do with them, I naturally want to do it perfectly. I diligently remind myself of this when it happens because I know it is important not to deny what I feel and validate my emotions. In other areas of my life, I would not say I slack off in giving my best; but I definitely give myself a break in feeling pressured to be perfect even in parenting.

Becoming your authentic self involves embracing your past cultural and family experience. As I said before, we should seek to endure the imperfections of our cultural heritage so we can be empowered toward transformational change. I definitely struggled with accepting my Korean culture; but here I am today, and I embrace it. This has been my transformation.

For instance, I saw that pieces of the Asian culture could enhance the overall experience of parenting and add value. Today, I feel one hundred percent Korean and one hundred percent American, which is amazing. Being bicultural is such an asset. Somehow, along the way, I adopted and adapted to what I really like about the Korean culture. For me to say I wish I could speak the Korean language fluently is saying a lot. I also seek to do a lot of things today to soak in Korean culture whenever I can. I know this creates a ripple effect not only in my work but also in my family.

My daughter after her first year in college came home

resentful, asking why we did not teach her the Korean language. I was pleasantly surprised to hear this but realized we may have raised our kids more American than we intended. After all, I am just now at the point where I fully embrace being a Korean American. I resonated with my daughter at that moment since I regret that I did not keep up with speaking Korean fluently. We told our kids it is never too late to learn the language and they can practice with their grandparents.

There is a certain comfort in accepting and embracing all of who you are. I know my kids have a healthy appreciation for Korean culture that I lacked when I was their age. They enjoy taking Korean food to school for lunch and are happy even sharing it with their friends because their friends love Korean food. This is wonderful to see, especially since I very much disliked associating myself with anything Korean when I was their age.

I want you to know that you can endure your struggles with your culture, family, and any other trauma you endured and still can come out strong, your resilience shining. People want things to be perfect and want to fully heal, making a clean cut from their past hurt. But you cannot just shake off everything you went through.

Your past experiences are now a part of you. But that does not mean you need to allow them to define you. It is a trigger you will need to use to build your confidence. Even though I am a licensed mental health professional, I still endure some of what I feel I lacked in my past. A positive way to view your past struggles is realizing that it allows you to come up with ways to learn new techniques for coping and helps continue to build your stress resilience.

In closing, my experiences taught me so much. I share only a portion of my story in this book. It is an ongoing journey since identity is not final. I admit that the tiger in me is proud to sit with her cubs and resist the roar.

If you are interested in learning more about my parenting and how I used my "secret weapon" to raise my four Korean-American children, stay tuned for my next book, which will focus only on parenting. Until then, be blessed and resist the roar.

Cultural Confidence™

A is for Authentic (Not for Anxieties or Straight A's) is Jeanie Chang's first book in a series titled Cultural Confidence™, based on her mental health framework and curriculum, Cultural Confidence™ (which, at the time of this writing, is in its final stages of the trademark process). Cultural Confidence™ promotes healthy emotionality through the powerful intersections of identity, mindfulness, resilience, and mental health.

Her second book in the series (on parenting) will soon follow, and her third book (on family and relationships) will be out later in 2021.

Jeanie innovates in the field of mental health through several unique initiatives. She founded the national "Self-Care & Wellness" program, which she created for business leaders and professionals. She also founded a nonprofit foundation, Authentic Self-Care & Wellness, Inc. Jeanie also has her own YouTube Channel, called "Noona's Noonchi," where she does a deep dive into Korean dramas from a mental health perspective.

Author Bio

Jeanie Chang is a Licensed Marriage and Family Therapist and Founder of Your Change Provider, PLLC, an interdisciplinary practice founded on solutions and cultural confidence™ in promoting good mental health and well-being.

She is an accomplished international speaker for corporations, communities, and colleges on topics such as burnout, resilience, mindfulness, stress, workplace well-being, trauma, and mental health conditions including anxiety, depression, and suicidality.

Jeanie is a Certified Mental Health Integrative Medicine Provider (CMHIMP) and Certified Clinical Trauma Professional (CCTP). She holds specialized training in Mindfulness Based Stress Reduction (MBSR). In addition, Jeanie is a corporate wellness and DEI consultant, executive leadership advisor, and family/parenting coach.

She followed a calling in mental health after a diverse career path. She first started as a broadcast journalist in Washington, DC, then went on to attend business school. Her work in the corporate sector includes marketing, public relations, and client success management.

Jeanie is an active volunteer in the Asian-American community. She enjoys serving as a clinical advisor for Asian-American mental health organizations around the country that focus on addressing mental health stigma and helping adolescents and families.

For her own self-care, Jeanie loves going out on dates with her husband of 23 years and planning family vacations. She and her husband have four children ages 13-20. Jeanie resides in Raleigh, North Carolina.

Acknowledgments

Thank you to my Apba and Umma (my parents) for their diligent hard work in parenting me. I am sure it was difficult, to say the least, in navigating a new culture, new school system, a new country, new everything as first-generation Korean Americans. I tend to forget you are immigrants because of how well you acculturated and speak English perfectly. Yes, it took me years to see this. I am very much appreciative and proud of who I am because of my upbringing.

Thank you, also, to my younger sister Kathy, whom I always admired growing up since she had to make up for my misgivings by being a good daughter to our parents. She came across more like the older sister, unnie, at times, for sure!

Thank you to the Council of Korean Americans (CKA) leaders and staff for our collaboration throughout the COVID-19 pandemic. It was our enriching work together to serve Korean Americans young and older, that inspired me to finally complete my book.

Thank you to my home church, Delaware Korean United Methodist Church (DKUMC), where I was blessed to find my path as a Christian. Special thanks to my fellow youth group besties for the fun times!

And last, thank you to Divya Parekh and her team for making my first book experience a wonderful one.

Made in the USA
Middletown, DE
02 May 2021